Watch Me Learn

Beginning Scissor Skills

3+

Editorial Project Manager
Mara Ellen Guckian

Editor in Chief
Brent L. Fox, M. Ed.

Creative Director
Sarah M. Fournier

Cover Artist
Diem Pascarella

Illustrators
Kevin Cameron
Amanda R. Harter

Imaging
Amanda R. Harter

Publisher
Mary D. Smith, M.S. Ed.

Teacher Created Resources
12621 Western Avenue
Garden Grove, CA 92841
www.teachercreated.com

ISBN: 978-1-4206-1713-9

©2022 Teacher Created Resources
Reprinted, 2025
Made in U.S.A.

Teacher Created Resources

Table of Contents

This book belongs to

Introduction

It's time to learn to cut and this book was designed to make cutting fun!

Children will progress from making little snips to cutting short lines. Each page builds on the skills practiced on the previous page, increasing the amount of cutting required.

After straight, curved, and zigzag lines have been explored, children will practice cutting shapes. Later, they will cut pieces using combinations of lines to create pictures or other projects.

Coloring is optional, but it is encouraged because it helps to develop fine motor skills, too. You might also wish to copy some of the pages onto colored paper for added interest. Additional materials children may wish to use to enhance the more advanced cutting practice pages include:

- crayons and markers
- glue sticks and tape
- colored paper (to copy pages)
- craft sticks
- craft materials
- toilet paper rolls

Choosing the Correct Scissors

Safety is important. Start with scissors that have rounded ends, but make certain that the scissors actually cut paper smoothly and easily to encourage students to keep practicing. Let your child try left- and right-handed scissors to see which is more comfortable. Be advised, they may change scissors and hands often before finding what works best for them.

How to Hold a Scissors

The small hole is for your thumb. Your thumb should be on top when holding the scissors. "Thumb up!"

Developing Cutting Skills

Pre-Cutting

Cutting skills require concentration, eye-hand coordination, and fine motor control. The *open-close movement* needed to use scissors requires children to build up the small muscles in their palms and fingers. These are the same muscles needed to hold pencils and pens to write.

Strengthening the muscles in a child's palms and fingers take time. There are many ways to help develop these muscles. Try the following activities:

- squeezing and rolling playdough or using "dough" scissors to cut the dough
- "pinching" using tongs and tweezers to pick up small toys, beans, or cotton balls
- "squeezing" with sponges, small squirt bottles, office tools such as hole punchers and staplers, "chip" clips, and clothespins with springs
- building with blocks that snap together
- using utensils when eating and holding a toothbrush when brushing their teeth

Introducing Scissors

To guide the paper or other material to be cut, children must be able to use one hand to cut and the other to hold and direct the item to be cut. (Hold the item, turn the item, and cut the item.) This *bilateral coordination* is not as easy as it sounds. The key is to start by making simple, short cuts or snips and build up as coordination and confidence improves.

1. First, practice holding the scissors correctly and use your thumb to open the scissors. Remind your child, "Thumb up!" The goal is to use the open-close motion with the cutting hand while moving the paper with the other hand.

2. Next, demonstrate opening the scissors and squeezing them closed. Have them do this over and over until they are comfortable with the motions.

3. Start by cutting straws or playdough "snakes" to get used to the open-close motion on something firm. Open the scissors. Slide the item to be cut into the "v" of the scissors, close the scissors on the item, and snip. Keep opening the scissors, moving to the "v," and closing the scissors each time. "Free-cutting" is a fun way to help children get comfortable using scissors.

4. Move on to *snipping* paper strips once children are adept at the open-close motion and comfortable holding the item to be cut. Try providing narrow strips of thin cardboard, craft foam, or colored index cards to make it fun. Paint chip samples are also great to use since the paper is a little sturdier than copy paper and the colors make it fun.

5. Be patient. It can take months to develop the muscles in a child's fingers and palms to establish the fine motor coordination needed to cut. Start slowly, use a variety of materials, and build up the amount of cutting as interest grows.

Sun, Moon, and Stars

Directions: Cut the five strips to separate them for your child. Encourage them to carefully cut the short, straight lines on each strip.

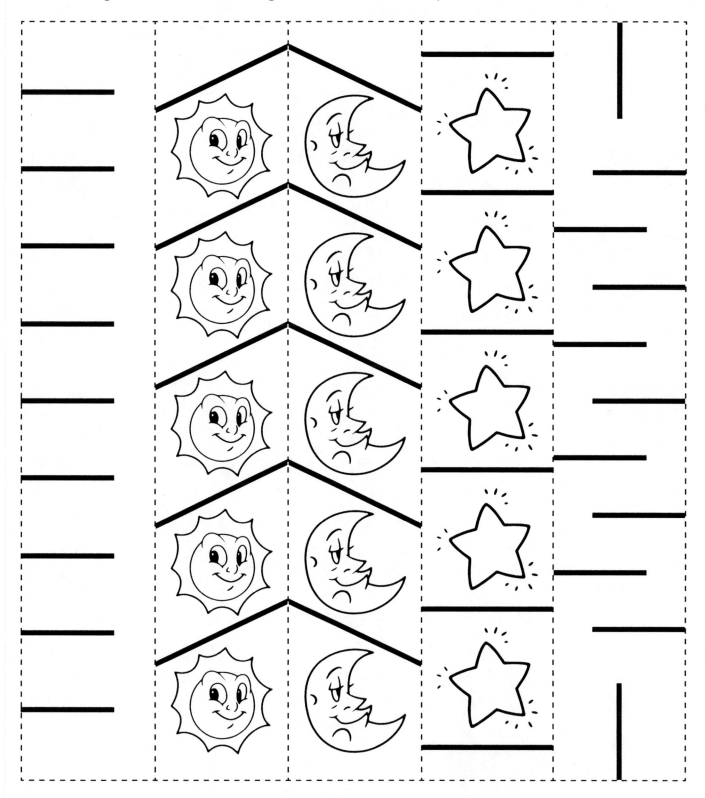

Suggestion: Use the pieces to create mosaics or collages.

All Kinds of Insects

Directions: Cut the six strips to separate them for your child. Encourage them to carefully cut the short, curved lines on each strip. Sort and count the insects.

Find Your Favorite Bird

Directions: Cut the two sections to separate them for your child. Encourage them to carefully cut along the longer straight lines to separate the birds.

Sea Creatures

Directions: Cut the two sections to separate them for your child. Have them carefully cut along the curvy lines to separate the sea creatures. Name each one.

Dinosaurs

Directions: Carefully cut along the long, straight lines to reach each dinosaur.

Time to STOP!

Directions: Carefully cut along the roads to reach the **STOP** signs.

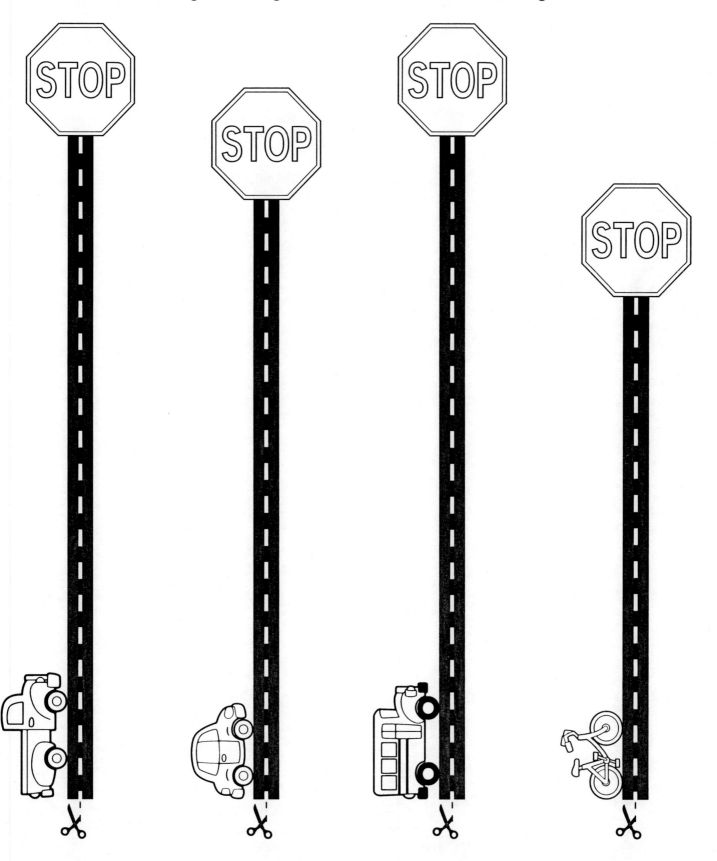

Time to Go Home

Directions: Carefully cut along the zig-zag lines to follow each animal's path.

Pirate Treasure

Directions: Carefully cut along the zig-zag lines to reach each pirate item.

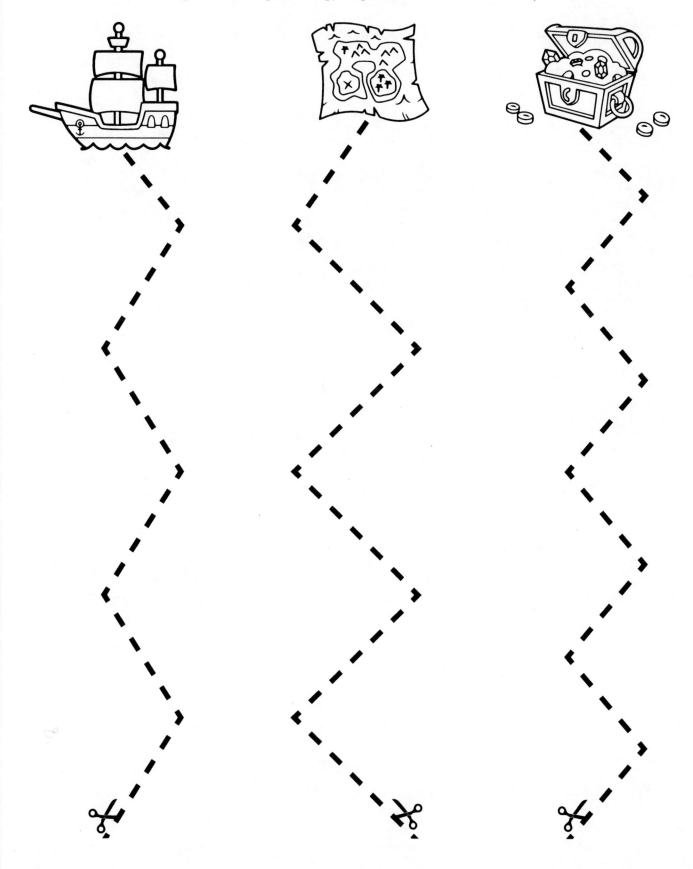

Hop, Walk, or Run?

Directions: Carefully cut along the long, curved lines to follow each animal's path.

Wild Animals

Directions: Carefully cut along the long, curved lines to reach each wild animal.

Flying High

Directions: Carefully cut along the different lines to reach each aircraft.

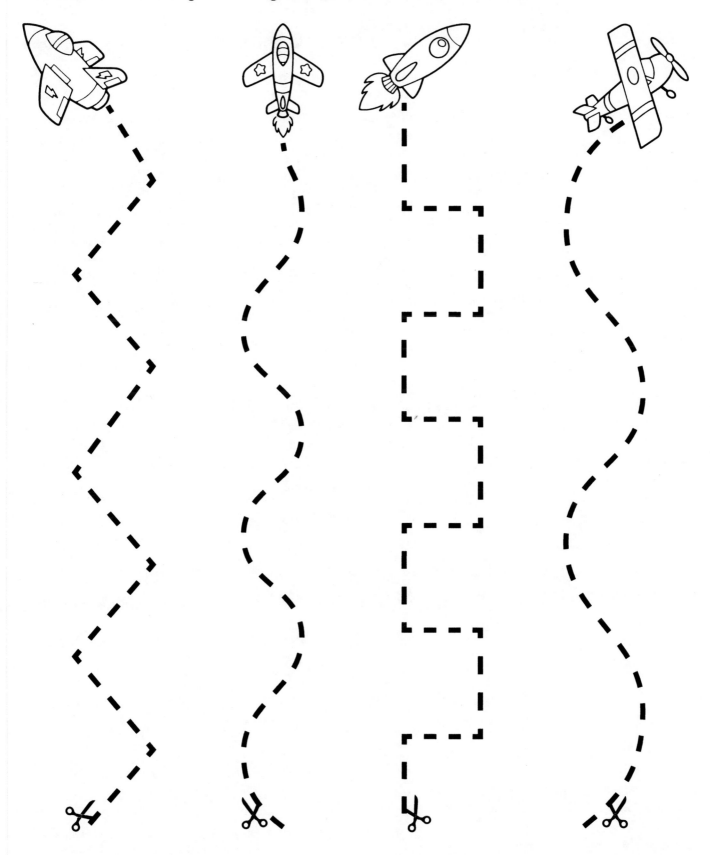

Build a Tower

Directions: Color each square and then carefully cut them out.

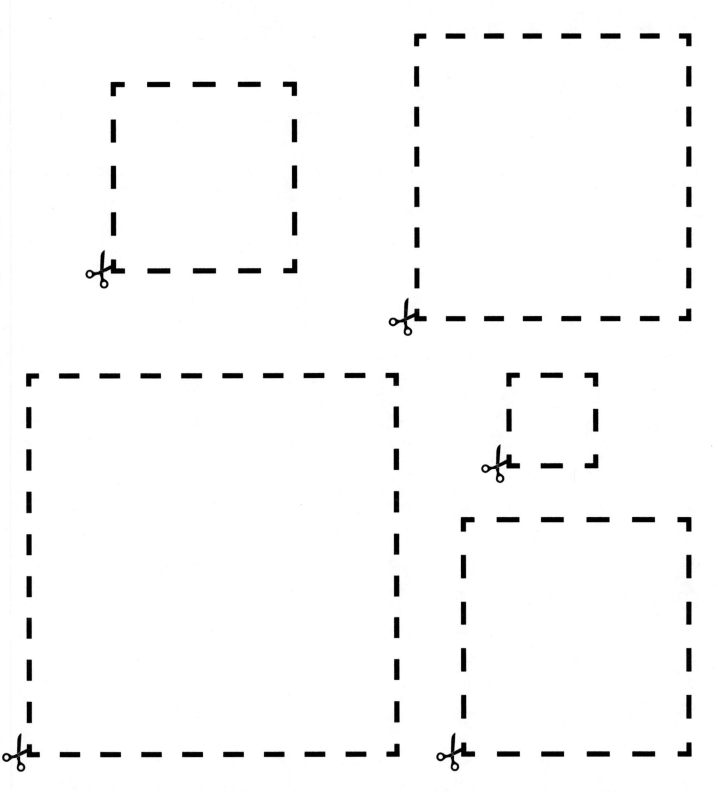

Suggestion: Stack the squares to make a tower. Once you have an arrangement you like, glue the tower to a sheet of paper. Add decorations.

Make a Cake

Directions: Carefully cut out the rectangles. Stack four rectangles to make a cake. Put the candle on top. Glue them onto a sheet of paper and decorate the cake.

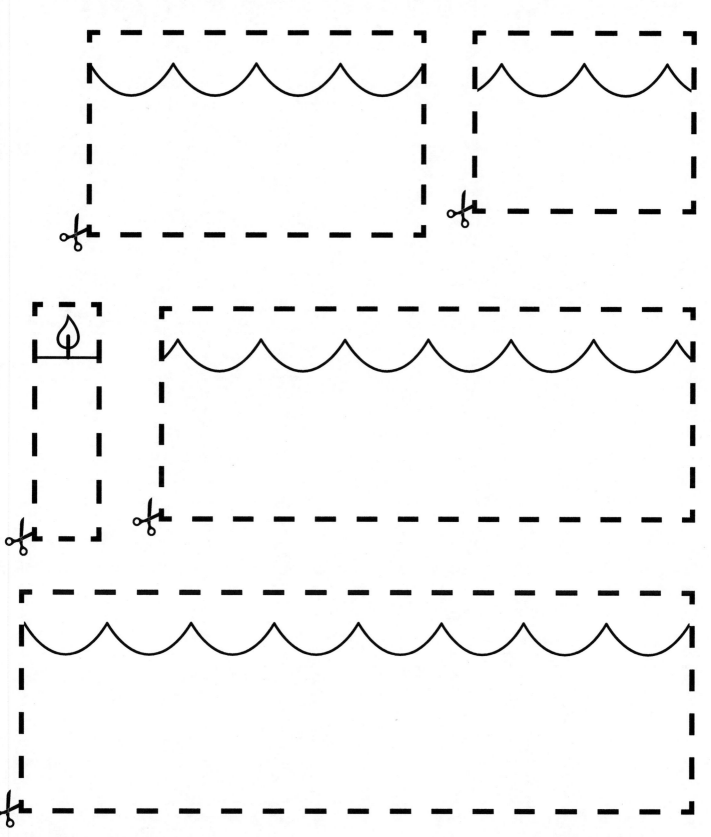

Pine Tree

Directions: Carefully cut out the three triangles and the small rectangle. Glue the trunk to the bottom of a sheet of paper. Glue the largest triangle to the trunk. Next, add the medium-sized triangle. The smallest triangle will be on top.

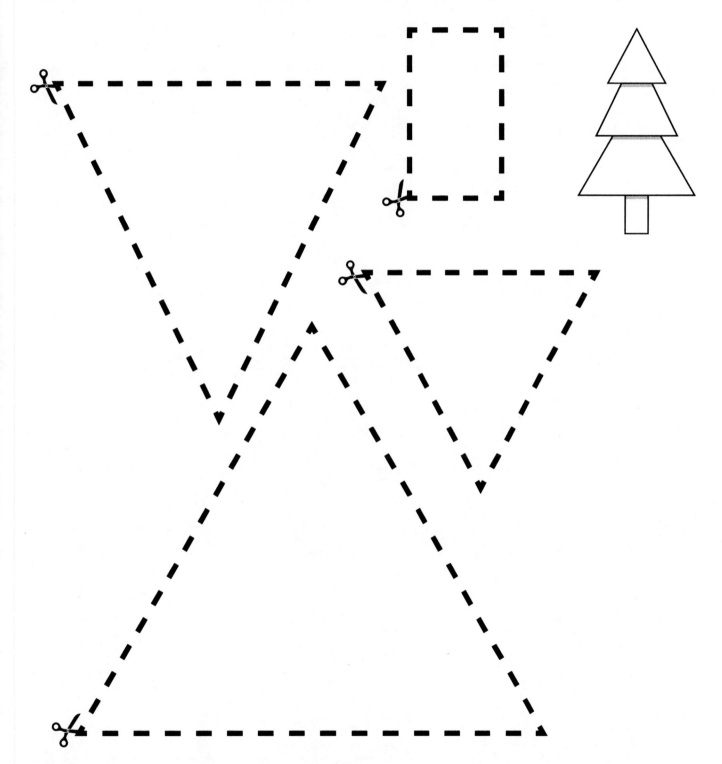

Suggestion: Color the tree and decorate it with pompoms and other craft items.

How Many Balls?

Directions: Color the balls and cut out each one. Do you have a favorite sport?

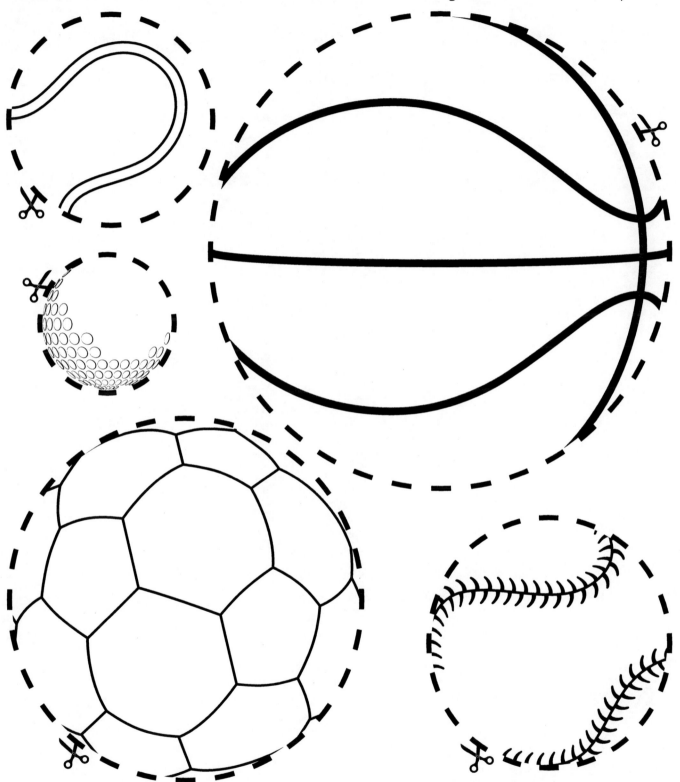

Suggestion: Arrange the balls in different ways—largest to smallest, smallest to largest, etc.

Eggs in the Nest

Directions: Color the nest and the eggs. Carefully cut out the eggs and glue them into the nest. What shape are the eggs?

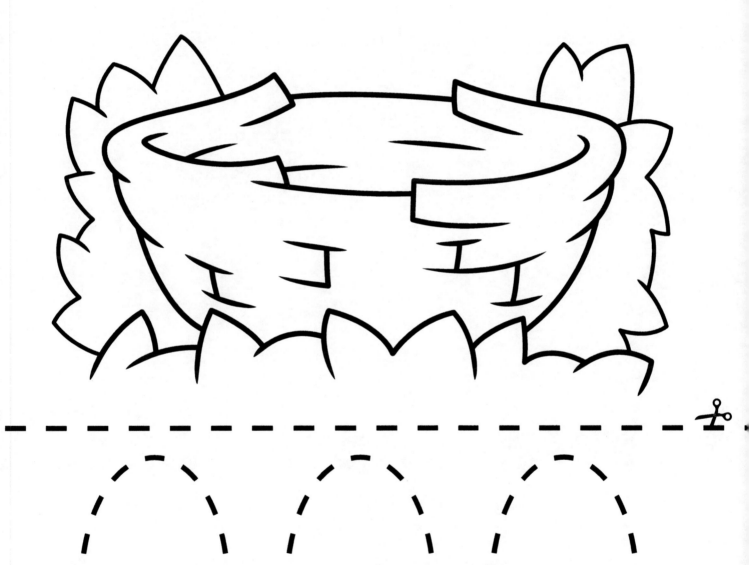

Smiling Stars

Directions: Draw happy faces on each star and then carefully cut them out.

Suggestion: Attach the stars to sticks or paint stirrers and make magic wands.

Happy Hearts

Directions: Color the happy hearts and then carefully cut them out.

Suggestion: Give each heart to a special person.

Gigantic Gems

Directions: Color the gems and then carefully cut them out. How many shapes can you name?

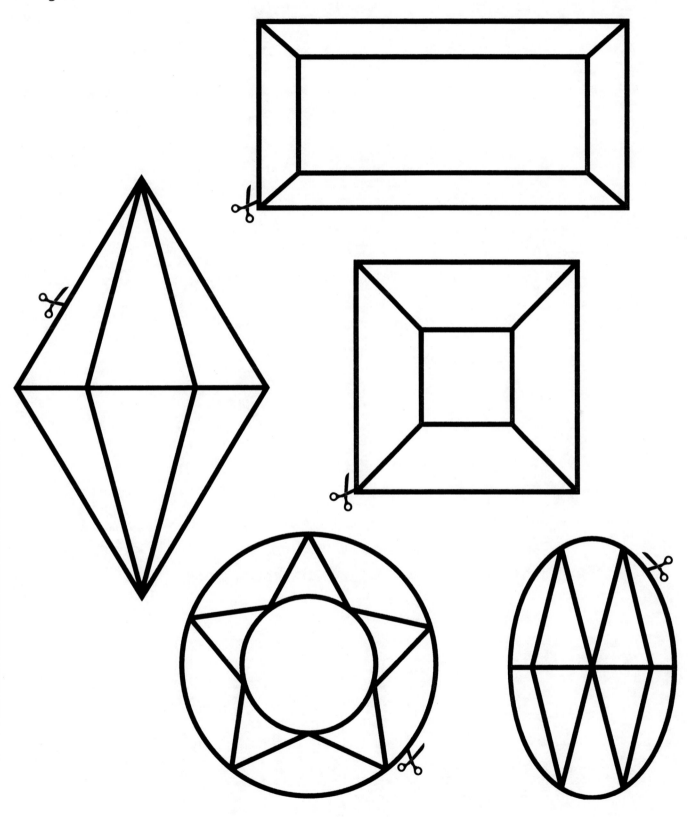

Monster Cookies

Directions: Color the cute monster cookies and then carefully cut them out.

Suggestion: Glue the cute monster cookies onto a paper plate.

Lion — Cut and Snip!

Directions: Color the lion's face and his mane. Then, carefully cut out the large circle. Snip the dashed lines to make the lion's mane.

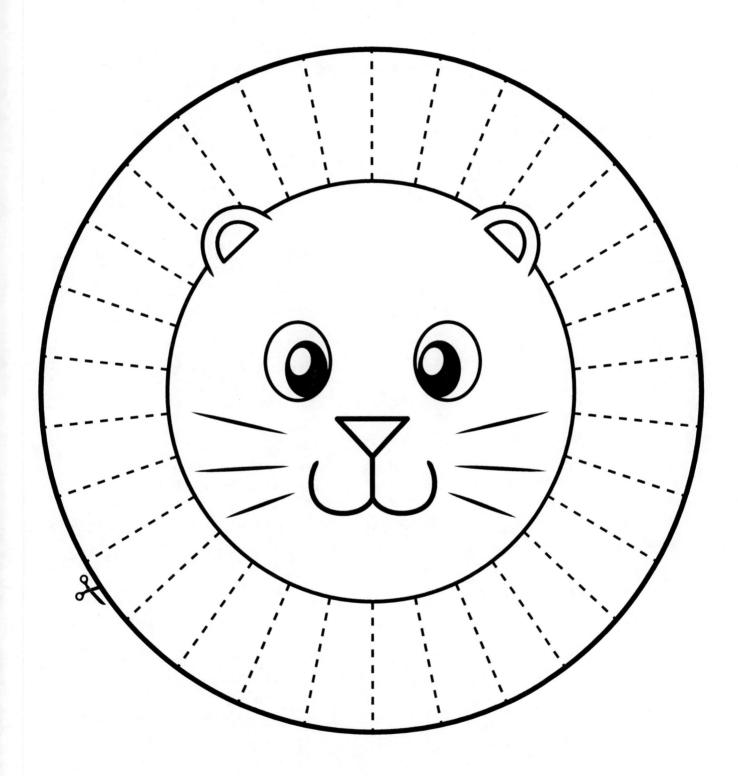

Happy Hedgehog

Directions: Color the hedgehog. Cut out the circle and fold it on the fold line. Glue the two halves together and let the hedgehog dry. Then, cut on the dashed lines to make the spines.

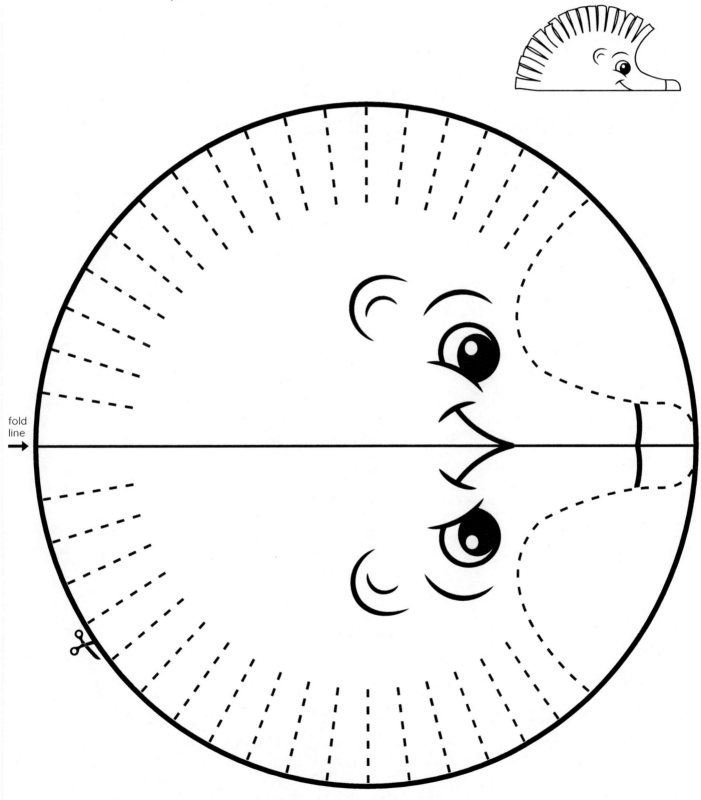

fold
line

Owl Fun

Directions: Color the owl and carefully cut it out. Then, cut the three zigzag lines on the body. Lay the pieces on a sheet of colored paper. Separate them so that the colored paper shows through. Draw wings and feet.

Make a Bunny

Directions: Color the bunny's two ears and face. Carefully cut out the pieces on the dashed lines and use tape to attach the ears to the head.

Make a Bear

Directions: Carefully cut out all eight pieces. Glue or tape the pieces together to make a bear. Color the bear.

Tulip Time

Directions: Carefully cut out the tulip flower, stem, and two leaves. Arrange the pieces and glue them to a sheet of paper. Color the tulip.

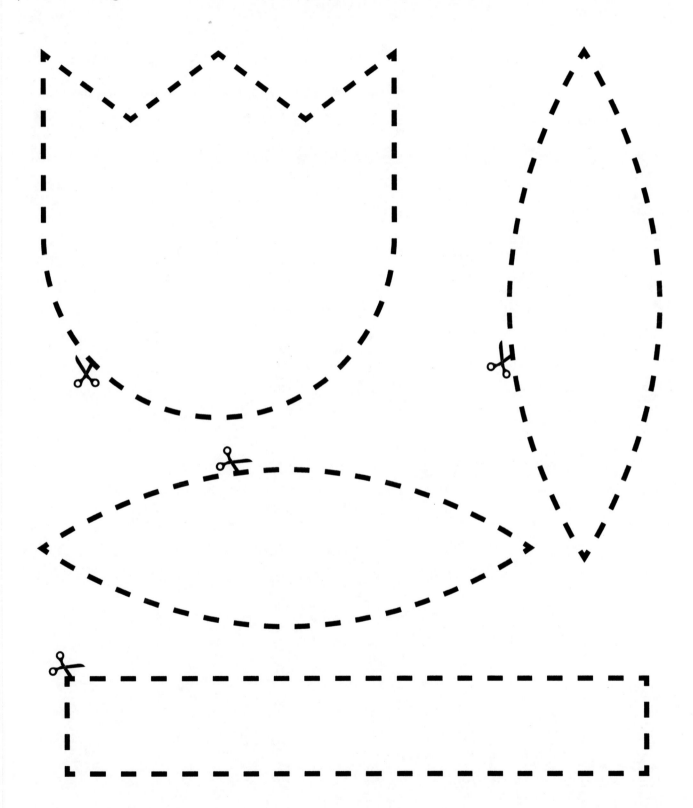

My Favorite Ice Cream

Directions: Color the cone and three ice cream scoops to show your favorite flavors. Carefully cut out the pieces and glue them to a sheet of paper.

Make a Gingerbread House

Directions: Carefully cut out the three pieces of the gingerbread house. Arrange the pieces and glue them to a sheet of paper. Color the house.

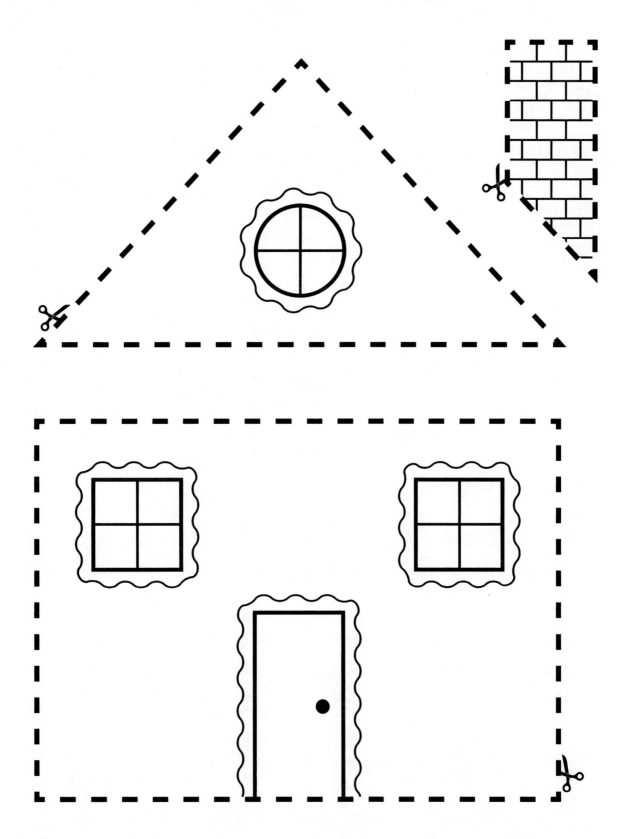

Build a Rocket

Directions: Carefully cut out the five pieces. Glue or tape the pieces together to make a rocket. Color the rocket.

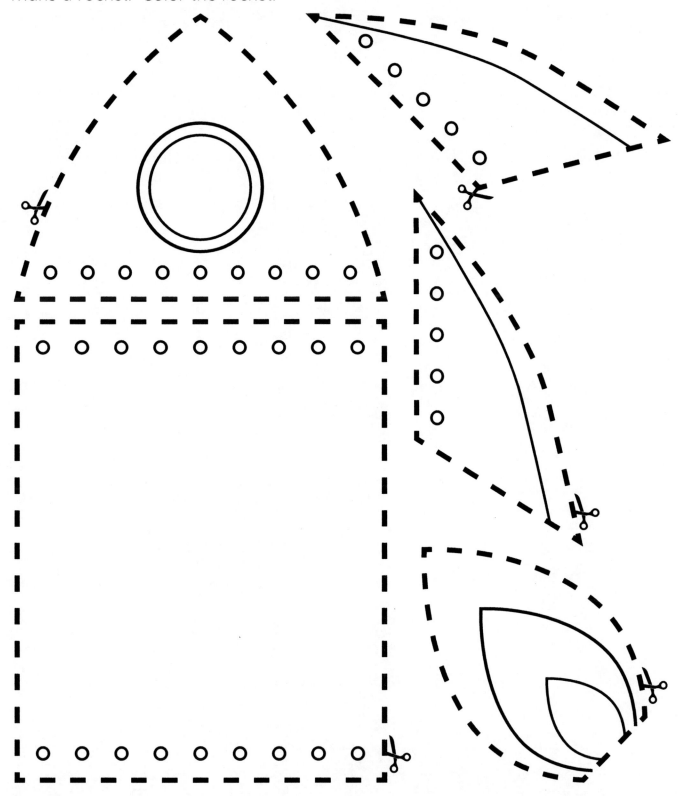

Suggestion: Tape the rocket to a craft stick and fly it around the room.

Friendly Fish

Directions: Carefully cut out the fish and glue on the tails. Color the fish.

Glue here.

Glue here.

Suggestion: Glue the fish onto blue paper. Add glitter or sparkles.

Jolly Jellyfish

Directions: Color the two pieces of the jellyfish. Carefully cut out the pieces. Snip the strips and curl them to make tentacles. Assemble the jellyfish.

Make a Pumpkin

Directions: Color the pumpkin, stem, and two leaves. Carefully cut out the pieces. Tape or glue the pieces of the pumpkin together.

Suggestion: Add a face to the pumpkin to make a jack-o-lantern.

Spider in a Web

Directions: Color the spider. Carefully cut out the web and the spider.

Suggestion: Glue the web to a paper plate and tape the spider to one end of a 15-inch piece of string. Tape the other end of the string to the bottom of the plate so that the spider can be moved on and off the web.

Make a Turkey

Directions: Color the body of the turkey and the eight feathers. Carefully cut out the pieces and attach the feathers to the turkey.

Snowman

Directions: Carefully cut out the five snowman parts and glue them onto a sheet of paper. Color the snowman.

Suggestion: Create a snow scene around the snowman.

Erupting Volcano

Directions: Carefully cut out the two parts of the volcano. Assemble them on a separate sheet of paper. Color the volcano.

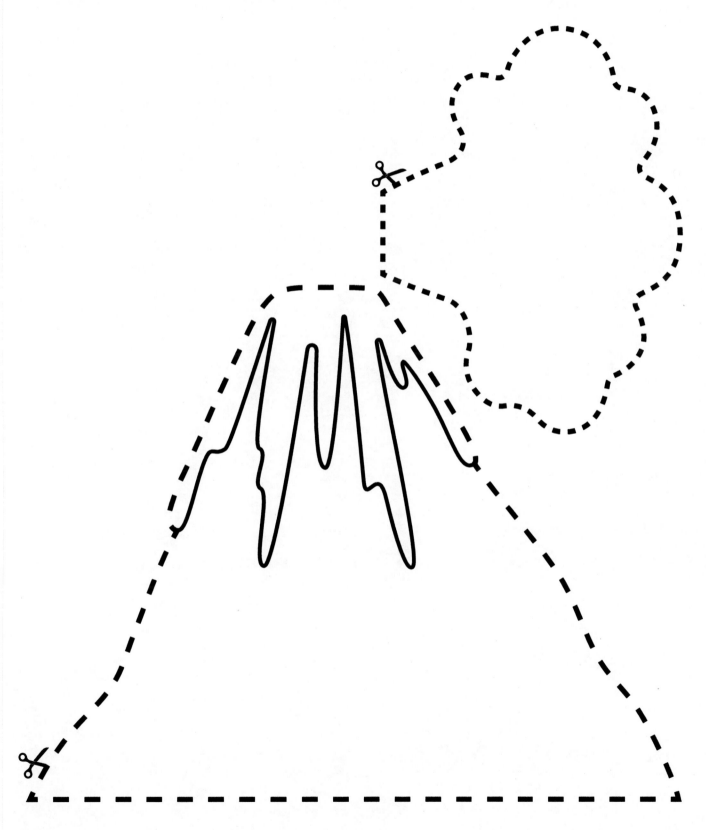

Paper Tube Puppet

Directions: Carefully cut out the four pieces. Cut the dashed lines to make thin strips on the largest piece. Wrap the large piece around a toilet paper tube. The thin strips will be the puppet's hair. Choose a face for the puppet and glue it on.

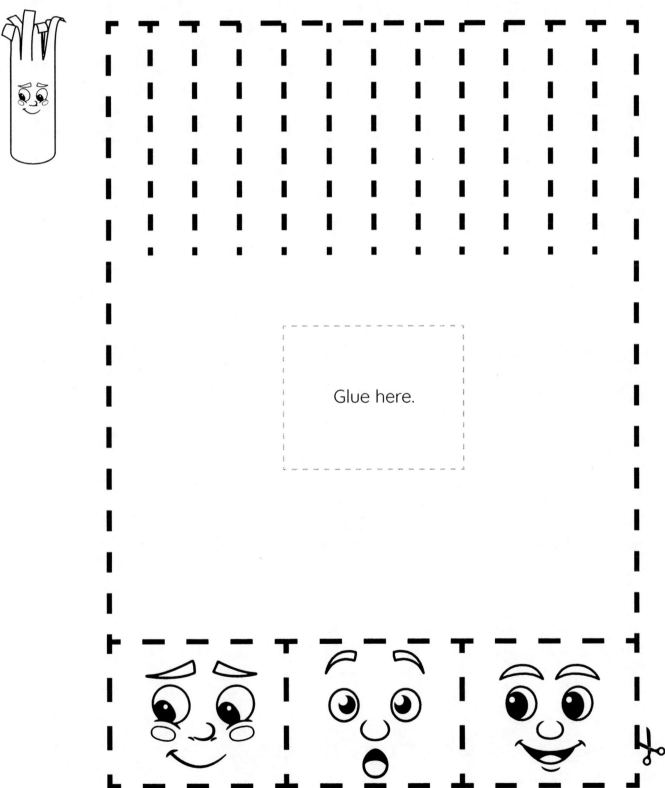

Glue here.

Land of Dinosaurs

Directions: Color the picture. Then, cut out the picture and cut along the dashed lines to make a puzzle. Can you put the pieces back together?